Ms. K's Kitchen

**This is the door
to Ms. K's kitchen.**

**This is the key
that opens the door
to Ms. K's kitchen.**

This is the key ring
that holds the key
that opens the door
to Ms. K's kitchen.

**This is Ms. K
holding the key ring
that holds the key
that opens the door
to Ms. K's kitchen.**

This is Ms. K's kitchen.

**This is Ms. K in her kitchen.
She's kind to her kitten.**